W9-AXZ-187

Portable Homes

Debbie Gallagher

Smart Apple Media

This edition first published in 2008 in the United States of America by Smart Apple Media.

Smart Apple Media
2140 Howard Drive West
North Mankato, Minnesota 56003

First published in 2007 by
MACMILLAN EDUCATION AUSTRALIA PTY LTD
627 Chapel Street, South Yarra, Australia 3141

Visit our Web site at www.macmillan.com.au or go directly to www.macmillanlibrary.com.au

Associated companies and representatives throughout the world.

Library of Congress Cataloging-in-Publication Data

Gallagher, Debbie, 1969-
Portable homes / by Debbie Gallagher.
p. cm. — (Homes around the world)
Includes index.
ISBN 978-1-59920-150-4
1. Tents—Juvenile literature. 2. Nomads—Juvenile literature. 3. Travelers—Juvenile literature.
I. Title.

TH4890.G345 2007
728.7'9—dc22

2007004641

Edited by Angelique Campbell-Muir
Text and cover design by Christine Deering
Page layout by Domenic Lauricella
Photo research by Legend Images
Illustration by Domenic Lauricella

Printed in U.S.

Acknowledgements
The author and the publisher are grateful to the following for permission to reproduce copyright material:

Cover photograph: Lavvu © Getty Images/Johner Images.

© age fotostock/Doug Scott, pp. 14, 24; © Images&Stories/Alamy, p. 8; © Colin Monteath/AUSCAPE, p. 21;
© Kevin Fleming/CORBIS/Australian Picture Library, pp. 6 (bottom), 16, 17, 18, 19; © Dreamstime.com, p. 4;
© Breck/Dreamstime.com, p. 30 (center left); © Brownm39/Dreamstime.com, p. 30 (bottom right); © Endostock/
Dreamstime.com, pp. 3, 5; © The DW Stock Picture Library, Sydney, p. 27; © Getty Images/Johner Images,
pp. 1, 15; © Getty Images/National Geographic/Gordon Wiltsie, p. 23; © Getty Images/Stone/Jorn Georg Tomter,
pp. 6 (center), 12, 13; © iStockphoto.com/Eric Bechtold, p. 30 (top right); © iStockphoto.com/Jacques Croizer,
p. 30 (top left); © iStockphoto.com/Janis Dreosti, pp. 7 (bottom), 25; © Lonely Planet Images/John Elk III, pp. 6
(top), 11; © Mark Moxon, www.moxon.net, pp. 9, 30 (bottom left); © Kevin Bubriski/Saudi Aramco World/PADIA,
p. 10; © Michael Spencer/Saudi Aramco World/PADIA, p. 30 (center right); © Nik Wheeler/Saudi Aramco World/
PADIA, pp. 7 (top), 20, 22; © Photolibrary/Plainpicture Gmbh & Co. Kg, p. 26.

While every care has been taken to trace and acknowledge copyright, the publisher tenders their apologies for
any accidental infringement where copyright has proved untraceable. Where the attempt has been unsuccessful,
the publisher welcomes information that would redress the situation.

Contents

Glossary words
When a word is printed in **bold**, you can look up its meaning in the glossary on page 31.

Shelter

Everyone needs shelter, as well as food and water, warmth, and protection. Homes around the world provide shelter for people.

Desert people need a home they can move from place to place.

People live in many different types of homes. People who move from place to place are called nomads. They live in portable homes.

Many modern travelers live in mobile homes.

Portable homes

Portable homes are easy to move around. There are many different types of portable homes.

Desert tents are home to the Tuareg in the Sahara Desert.

The Sami, in Scandinavia, live in lavvu.

Nomads in Somalia live in aqals.

People build portable homes to suit the conditions of the place they live in. The place may be hot or cold, wet or windy.

Many people across central Asia live in yurts.

People all around the world live in mobile homes.

Desert tent

The Tuareg people live in desert tents. The Tuareg are nomads who raise **livestock** in the Sahara Desert. Desert tents can be easily moved.

Nomadic families move their livestock around with them.

A desert tent is made by placing coverings over bent wooden poles. They are tied down with ropes so they do not blow away.

roof of woven mats

poles

ropes

mat walls

open doorway

Goatskin or woven mats are used for covering the tents.

Inside a desert tent

Inside a desert tent parents sleep on a bed. Children sleep on mats on the ground. Cooking is done on an open fire outside or in a separate tent.

belongings tied to pole

wooden frame

woven mat walls

There is a lot of space inside a desert tent.

floor mats

The tent walls can be opened or closed. When a storm begins, they are closed to keep the sand and fierce winds out.

Tent walls can be opened to let in cool breezes.

Lavvu

Lavvu are tents used in **arctic** places where it is very cold and windy. The Sami are the **indigenous people** of northern Scandinavia. Many of them are nomads who raise herds of reindeer.

Lavvu provide shelter for the Sami people.

The frame is made by leaning strong poles against each other. It is covered with two layers of reindeer skins. This makes the lavvu **waterproof**.

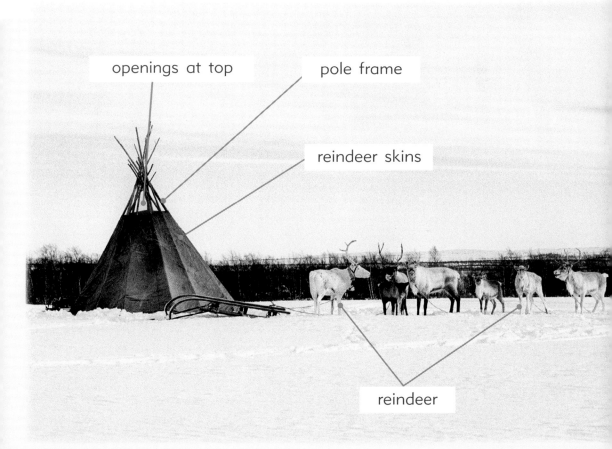

openings at top

pole frame

reindeer skins

reindeer

Even when it snows, it is warm inside a lavvu.

Inside a lavvu

Inside a lavvu, seating can be changed into beds for the family to sleep in. The family sits around the edge of the **hearth** to eat.

mats on floor

cooking pot

kettle

An open fire is used for cooking and warmth.

The Sami have lived in lavvu for hundreds of years. Some Sami now use tent canvas instead of reindeer skins to make lavvu.

A fire keeps the home warm inside.

Aqal

An aqal is a portable hut used in Somalia in eastern Africa. Many Somalis are nomads who keep herds of animals.

Somali nomads move around the desert looking for food and water for their animals.

Aqals are dome-shaped huts. The frame is made from the roots of acacia trees. Then it is covered with woven mats or animal skins.

frame made from acacia tree roots

acacia trees

woven mat floor

Somali women put up the family's aqal at each stopping place.

Inside an aqal

Inside an aqal, screen walls separate different areas. The sleeping area is at the back. The living area is at the front. Cooking is done on a hearth outside.

open doorway

woven mats

grain used for food

Grain is pounded for food outside the aqal.

An aqal protects the family from extreme desert temperatures. Aqals are made from local materials, and last for many years of traveling.

Groups of families travel together and set up their aqals next to each other.

Yurt

A yurt is a circular tent used by nomadic families across areas of central Asia. The mountain areas are often very cold, but the yurts are warm inside.

Each yurt has a hole in the top to let light in and smoke out.

Yurts are made by tying coverings to a circular **lattice frame**. The hole in the top can be covered during bad weather.

roof ring

roof poles

lattice frame

The roof ring and lattice frame give the yurt its circular shape.

Inside a yurt

Inside a yurt, there is a stove or open fire. This is used for cooking and to keep the home warm.

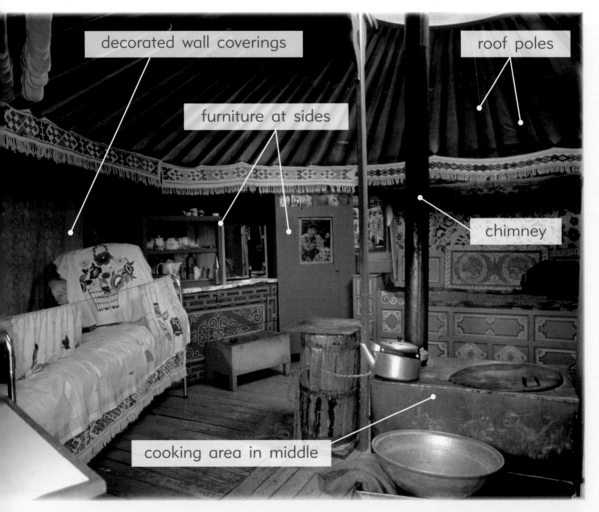

decorated wall coverings

roof poles

furniture at sides

chimney

cooking area in middle

Beds and other furnishings are placed around the inside walls.

Yurts can be made larger by adding more sections to the walls. More coverings can add warmth. In summer, the layers can be lifted to let in the breezes.

The roof ring is the most important part of a yurt.

Mobile home

A mobile home is a home on wheels. **Traditional** mobile homes are pulled by horses. Modern mobile homes are towed by cars or trucks.

In France, this family lives and travels in a traditional mobile home.

24

Some families who move around a lot choose to live in mobile homes. Traditional travelers such as the Roma people of Europe live in mobile homes called caravans.

windows

driving lights at back

wheel

towbar attaches to car or truck

Circus performers live in mobile homes.

Inside a mobile home

Inside a mobile home, there is a kitchen. The seats fold out into beds. Bigger mobile homes also have a bathroom.

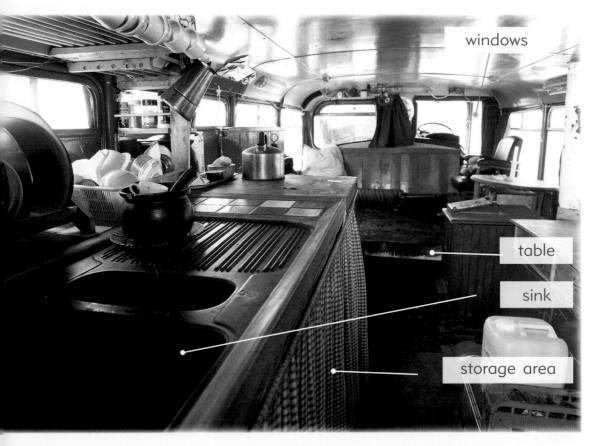

windows

table

sink

storage area

A mobile home has many of the same features as a permanent home.

A pop-up roof makes a mobile home bigger inside.
An **awning** can also be added to the outside.
An awning gives the family more living space.

An awning can provide shade on a hot day.

Floor plan

This is the **floor plan** of an aqal. It gives you a "bird's-eye view" of the rooms inside the home.

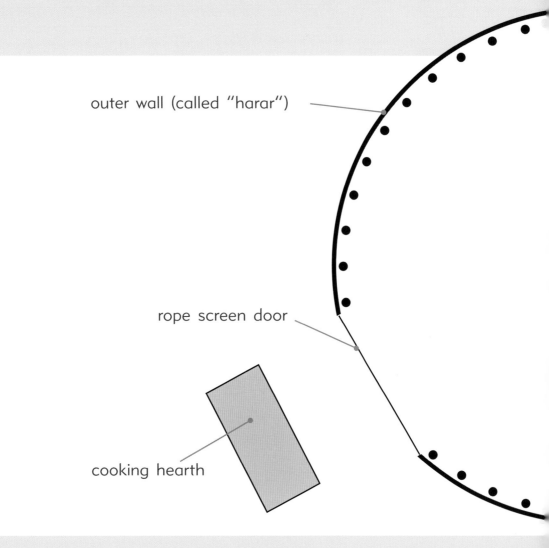

outer wall (called "harar")

rope screen door

cooking hearth

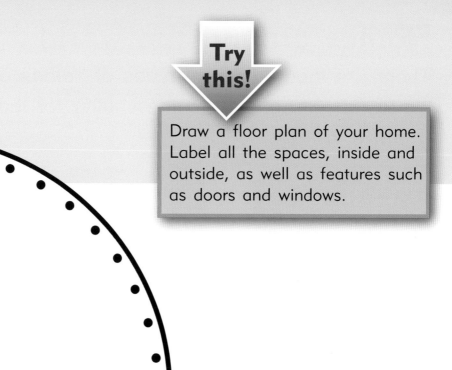

Try this!

Draw a floor plan of your home. Label all the spaces, inside and outside, as well as features such as doors and windows.

sleeping area

acacia-wood frame poles

inside screen wall

Homes around the world

There are many different types of homes around the world. All homes provide shelter for the people who live in them.

A pit home in Africa

New York City apartments

Windsor Castle in London

Mud and grass homes

Tuareg tent in the Sahara Desert

Lake home in Asia

Glossary

arctic
the region around the North Pole

awning
a covering, like a roof, that extends from the side of a mobile home

floor plan
a drawing that shows the layout of the areas in a home or building, as if seen from above

hearth
part of the floor where a fire is made or cooking is done

indigenous people
people native to a particular area or country

lattice frame
a frame made by crossing strips of wood or other material

livestock
animals, such as horses, cattle, sheep, goats, or camels, that are kept by farmers

traditional
used for a long time by a particular people or in a particular area

waterproof
something that does not allow water through

Index